THE

AARONIC

PRIESTHOOD

PROPERTY OF:

_____

THE

AARONIC

PRIESTHOOD

A GUIDE FOR
YOUNG MEN

THOMAS E. JOHNSON

CFI
An Imprint of Cedar Fort, Inc.
Springville, Utah

ISBN 13: 978-1-4621-1689-8

Published by CFI, an imprint of Cedar Fort, Inc.
2373 W. 700 S., Springville, UT 84663
Distributed by Cedar Fort, Inc., www.cedarfort.com

LIBRARY OF CONGRESS CATALOGING-IN-PUBLICATION DATA

Johnson, Thomas E., 1948- author.
The Aaronic Priesthood : a guide for young men / Thomas E. Johnson.
    pages cm
ISBN 978-1-4621-1689-8 (perfect bound : alk. paper)
1. Aaronic Priesthood (Mormon Church) 2. Mormon boys--Religious life. 3. Church of Jesus Christ of Latter-day Saints--Doctrines. 4. Mormon Church--Doctrines. I. Title.

 BX8659.5.J64 2015
 262'.149332--dc23

                        2015024330

Cover design by Shawnda T. Craig
Cover design © 2015 Lyle Mortimer
Edited and typeset by Kevin Haws

Printed in China

10 9 8 7 6 5 4 3 2 1

Printed on acid-free paper

CONTENTS

INTRODUCTION

Dear Young Man,

What do you want to be when you grow up?

Maybe you have thought about becoming a doctor, lawyer, teacher, veterinarian, sports coach, scientist, policeman, computer programmer, engineer, banker, construction worker, architect, oil driller, fireman, or some other occupation.

While any of these occupations are good, have you thought about becoming a righteous man of God, a priest of God, and a teacher of the gospel of Jesus Christ?

A righteous man learns about God. God is the Father of your spirit, which gives life to your body (so He is often referred to as our "Heavenly Father"). A righteous man also learns about God's son, Jesus

Christ, who came to earth and taught people how to become righteous. A righteous man teaches others how to become like God. A righteous man is a man who learns about God's love for His children and is a good influence on his family, friends, and all the people he meets. He is a leader and good example for his wife and children.

Because he does these good things, he is loved by God, and God blesses him and gives him power to do many good things.

When God shares His power with men, it is called the priesthood. When a man holds the priesthood, he has authority to represent God and do His work on the earth.

For example, with the priesthood, a man can perform ordinances. These are ceremonies, like baptism, that help people come closer to God. The priesthood gives a man influence when used well because good people respect and honor him and try to be like him. He can receive and help others receive eternal life.

Eternal life is what we can get as our reward after we die if we have kept the rules and commandments of God. Someday, we will all die, but later, when Jesus comes to this earth again to live here, we will all be resurrected. *Resurrected* means to live again after we die, with a body that cannot die ever again. Those people who obeyed the commandments when they

were alive will be happy and live with God, Jesus Christ, and the other righteous people. That is what it means to receive eternal life. Those who didn't obey the commandments of God and didn't repent while they were alive will not have a happy life after they die. They will have to suffer for their sins for a long time and will be separated from the righteous people.

The things you prepare to do by study and training will be your occupation—your job—during your life. You need to learn an occupation so you can work, earn money, and support yourself and your family. No one can become a doctor, lawyer, engineer, scientist, or any of the various occupations without study and training.

You also need to study and train in order to become a righteous man. You have to learn what God wants you to do and how to do it. When you die, it won't matter what your occupation was (as long as it was honest work), but it will greatly matter whether you were a righteous man.

WHERE DO I START?

You begin your journey to become a righteous man by preparing for baptism to become a member of The Church of Jesus Christ of Latter-day Saints. You need to learn about God and His Son, Jesus Christ—who They are, what They are like, and what They want you to know and do. You need to learn to pray to God. You need to repent, which means you have to stop doing bad things and start doing good things.

Jesus was baptized by a man named John the Baptist. Jesus wants all of us to get baptized too. When you get baptized, you are making a promise to remember God and Jesus Christ each day and to try to become like Them by following Their rules and commandments. After you are baptized, older men holding the Melchizedek Priesthood will put their hands on your

© Simon Dewey. Used by permission.

head and bless you with the gift of the Holy Ghost (sometimes called the Holy Spirit).

When you are baptized, any mistakes you have made and sins you have committed are forgiven by God. You become clean again, like you were when you were a baby before you did anything wrong. The Holy Ghost will help you make decisions each day of your life to choose to do good things and be a good person.

If you have learned these things in your family or by going to Primary at church on Sundays, you can be baptized when you are eight years old. Some people aren't ready at the age of eight and are baptized when they are older, but waiting longer means they don't get the gift of the Holy Ghost to help them (since they didn't receive it) until they are baptized.

After you turn eight years old, you are responsible for the choices you make. Making good choices leads to blessings and making bad choices leads to suffering and unhappiness. By studying the scriptures and going to church, you can learn what the good choices are and how best to choose them.

When you turn eight, the devil (called Satan) tries to put ideas into your mind and influence you to make bad choices. This is called temptation. During this time in your life, it is important for you to learn how to make good choices and fight against temptation. The devil is real, but he can't hurt you or make you choose bad things unless you let him.

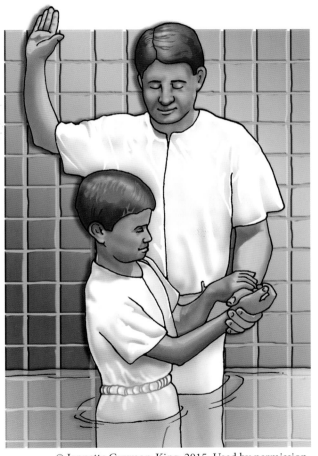

© Jennette Guymon-King, 2015. Used by permission.

RECEIVING THE PRIESTHOOD

Once you are a member of the Church, the next step on your path to becoming a righteous man is to receive the priesthood. When you receive the priesthood, you further your service to God and learn more about His work on the earth.

If you want to get to know God and become a righteous man, you can receive the priesthood when you are twelve years old. Sometimes, some people aren't ready to receive the priesthood at that time, and the bishop might ask them to wait for a while and try harder to live God's commandments before receiving the priesthood. One good way to prepare for receiving the priesthood is going to a "priesthood preview" when you are eleven. This is a meeting to tell boys more about the priesthood.

If you want to receive the priesthood, you should talk to your bishop. The bishop or one of his counselors will interview you—this means he will have a private meeting with you to talk about the priesthood. He will talk with you about God (our Heavenly Father) and Jesus Christ and about making a promise to follow Their commandments. He will ask you if you have been doing the things you promised to do when you got baptized—praying, going to Church meetings on Sunday, reading the scriptures, keeping your body clean and free from alcohol or tobacco or drugs, using clean language when you speak, being honest (not lying, cheating, or stealing), being chaste in your actions and pure in your mind and thoughts, and paying your tithing. This is called a worthiness interview.

If the bishop agrees that you are ready to receive the priesthood, he will say your name in a Sunday sacrament meeting and ask all the members present to raise their hand if they agree you should receive the priesthood. This is referred to as being sustained. After that, the bishop will choose a time and a place for you to receive the priesthood.

You can invite your family and close friends to watch you receive the priesthood. The bishop, your father, or someone the bishop chooses will place his hands on your head and confer the priesthood on

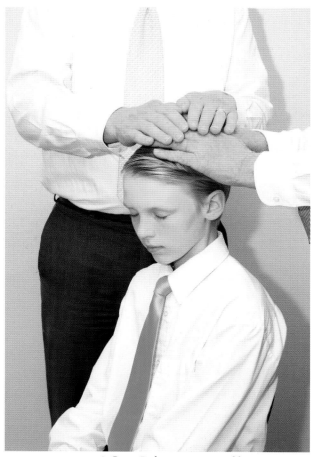

you, and you will be ordained to an office in the priesthood. Within a couple of weeks, you should receive a certificate showing that you were ordained. You should keep this certificate in your home with your other important papers.

The priesthood is the power to do good on earth. This usually means helping others—we call this priesthood service. When you are doing things that help only yourself, you are being selfish. Priesthood service is about helping other people and learning to be unselfish. God and Jesus Christ are unselfish, and we are learning to be like Them.

THE TWO PRIESTHOODS

There are two priesthoods. The first is called the Aaronic Priesthood. It's called this after a man named Aaron. Aaron lived a long time ago and was a brother to the great prophet Moses. God told Moses to put Aaron in charge of the tabernacle, which was the place where people who believed in God and wanted to serve Him came to worship. The tabernacle was like the temples we have in the Church today, but it was smaller and could be moved around from place to place.

The second priesthood is called the Melchizedek Priesthood. It is a higher priesthood, and God gives more authority and power to men who receive this priesthood. You must be a very good person to receive this priesthood. You will learn about the Melchizedek

Restoration of the
Aaronic Priesthood

Priesthood and prepare to receive it by receiving and participating in the Aaronic Priesthood.

The priesthood is necessary to establish and build up God's Church. About two hundred years ago, God and His Son, Jesus Christ, came to visit Joseph Smith. Joseph Smith wanted to be a righteous man and he had read the Bible and prayed to know what he should do. God and Jesus Christ called him to be a prophet leader of Their work on the earth.

John the Baptist, the same man who baptized Jesus when He lived on earth, was sent to visit Joseph Smith and Oliver Cowdery. He laid his hands on their heads and gave them the Aaronic Priesthood.

Later, Peter, James, and John, who were chosen by Jesus Christ to be leaders in His Church, came to Joseph and Oliver and gave them the Melchizedek Priesthood.

We have the priesthood in the Church today. Our priesthood leader is Jesus Christ. Those who follow Him and try to be like Him—including the prophet of the Church, the Twelve Apostles, the General Authorities (high leaders), and local leaders such as the bishop, his counselors, and the Young Men leaders—hold this priesthood authority to do God's work.

© Thomas E. Johnson, 2015.

BECOMING A DEACON

As you already know, when the Aaronic Priesthood is conferred upon you, you are ordained to an office in that priesthood. The first office is called a deacon. A deacon has authority to perform certain parts of God's work.

For example, a deacon is allowed to pass the sacrament (bread and water) in sacrament meeting on Sundays. Taking the sacrament is one of the ways God has asked us to worship Him, and it is the most important thing we do each week when we come to church.

It is a great honor to pass the sacrament because God has promised that those who come to church and take the sacrament worthily will always have the gift of the Holy Ghost with them. Each Sunday, when

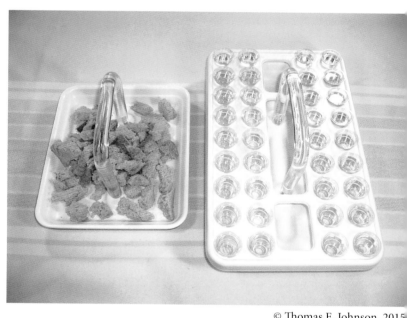

many people come to church, you will be giving them the blessing of receiving the Holy Ghost that week by your priesthood service in passing the sacrament. Now, you can see how your priesthood service is a blessing to other people.

Don't worry about how to pass the sacrament. When you go to church on Sundays, your priesthood leaders will teach you what to do.

The sacrament is so important that sometimes those who are old or sick and cannot come to church on Sundays will ask the bishop to bring the sacrament to them in their homes. The bishop or the Young Men's president might ask you to go with an older boy who is a priest or a man who is a Melchizedek Priesthood holder to take the sacrament to such people in their homes.

Another thing a deacon can do is serve as a messenger for the bishop. Sometimes the bishop will need to tell someone something and might write a note and ask a deacon to take it to that person. He trusts you not to read the note or share it with any other people.

Or, on fast Sundays, when people share their testimonies, the bishop might ask a deacon to take the microphone around to each person who wants to say his or her testimony.

Also, a deacon may be asked to gather fast offerings. In the Church, God cares about the poor and needy members—these are people who don't have enough money for their lives. God asks the Church members to give money each month to help these people. This money is given on the first Sunday of the month, the same Sunday when we fast (meaning to go without food and water for two meals), so this money is called fast offerings.

Where there are many members of the Church who live close together, the bishop may ask the deacons to go to visit members and give them an envelope so that if they want to give money (an offering) to help the poor, they can do so. The deacons always go together, two by two, walking in the neighborhood or sometimes an older Melchizedek Priesthood holder will drive them in a car. In some places where members live far apart, or there aren't enough Melchizedek Priesthood holders to help out, deacons don't collect fast offerings; instead, the members are asked to give their fast offerings with their tithing when they come to church on Sundays.

When the deacons do collect fast offerings, they bring them back to church and give them to one of the counselors in the bishopric, and then these donations are written in the records of the Church.

Deacons also help with taking care of the church building and the grounds. Sometimes, this will mean helping pick up the garbage to keep the building clean,

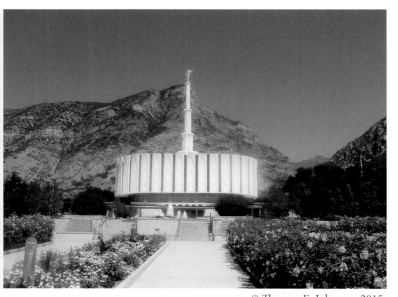

erasing the blackboards, putting paper towels or toilet paper in the bathrooms, cleaning windows, shoveling snow on the sidewalks in the winter, or any other tasks the bishop asks the deacons to do.

Becoming a man means learning how to work. If you do all of these things cheerfully, God will be pleased and will give you blessings in your life.

One of the most exciting new things you can do as a deacon is to go to the temple to do baptisms for the dead. You were baptized yourself, so you already know what baptism is. Many Church members do family history research to find out who their ancestors are, and the Church also does research to identify these people. These names are submitted to the temple, and people who go to the temple can be baptized for them. These people have already died and their bodies are buried in the earth, but their spirits are still alive and waiting in the spirit world for the resurrection. Some of these are people who never knew about the gospel of Jesus Christ or never had a chance to be baptized when they were living on the earth.

Because they don't have a body right now, they can't be baptized in the spirit world, but we can be baptized for them. We call this proxy baptism. If these people study and learn about the gospel of Jesus Christ in the spirit world and decide they want to be more righteous and be baptized, Jesus has said

© Rick Satterfield, 2004. Used by permission.

that the baptisms we do for them in the temple will count as if they had been baptized while they were still alive.

Your bishop and youth leaders will plan temple trips for the young people in your ward, so you will have a chance to go. You will need to have another interview to make sure you are worthy because God has said that if we go to the temple when we are not worthy, His Holy Spirit will not be there.

The temple is a beautiful place. This is probably your first chance to go inside the temple and learn what it is like. Someday, if you continue to be worthy, you can go to the temple to receive your endowment ordinance and to be married.

Even though you are still young, God welcomes you to the temple so you can feel the power of His Holy Spirit there. You will be giving priesthood service to help people be baptized who cannot be baptized for themselves.

When you become a deacon, you begin attending some new meetings on Sunday. You used to attend Primary, but now you will attend a Sunday School class (for twelve- and thirteen-year-old girls and boys) and priesthood meeting.

At the beginning of each priesthood meeting, you will be together with the older men for a few minutes, and then you will separate into your priesthood

THE AARONIC PRIESTHOOD

classes. These are called quorums—this means all the deacons are together. You will have an adult priesthood leader called the Young Men president, and he will have two counselors. One of the counselors is the adviser to the deacons quorum. Also, one of the bishop's counselors will be with you in your quorum meeting on Sundays.

In your meeting, the deacons quorum adviser or another person will be your teacher each Sunday. In this class, you will learn about the gospel, the priesthood, and many things to help you grow up and prepare to be a righteous man. You should make friends with the other deacons in your quorum; they can help you, and you should serve them by trying to help them in return.

As a priesthood holder, it's now time to dress properly. When you go to church on Sundays, you should always wear your best clothing to show respect for God. When you receive the priesthood, you are representing God and you should dress in a respectable way. This means a white shirt, tie, dark pants, and dark socks and shoes. If you have a suit or dark jacket, you should wear that. You should keep these clothes clean and check them each Saturday to make sure they are washed and ready for Sunday.

As an Aaronic Priesthood holder, you will learn about the Duty to God program. This is a series of

28

© Thomas E. Johnson, 2015.

activities that you can do to become more righteous and live the gospel of Jesus Christ. You will be given a booklet that you can use for several years to plan your activities and record your work.

You will also be given a booklet called *For the Strength of Youth*, written by the leaders of the Church; it teaches about the values and standards of God's Church and how to follow His teachings. You should also receive a copy of the booklet *True to the Faith: A Gospel Reference*. Ask for these booklets from your quorum adviser.

You'll also be old enough to start attending Mutual. Mutual is an activity meeting one night each week, lasting about one and a half hours. In most places, the Mutual activity follows the program of the Boy Scouts. Scouting is a program used throughout the world to help boys become good men.

If you've participated in Cub Scouts, you already know a lot about Scouting. A lot of Scouting is about outdoor activities such as hiking, camping, cooking, first aid, compass reading, and so on. But one of the best parts of Scouting is merit badges. Merit badges are short study classes about many different subjects. There are over 130 merit badges to choose from. By using merit badge books and meeting with merit badge counselors, you can learn about numerous different

topics. These can be really helpful to you to find out what you might want to do as an occupation when you grow up.

There are different levels of Scouting called ranks. You will start out as a Tenderfoot and can advance to Second Class, First Class, Star, Life, and then Eagle, the top rank. Your Scout leader, called the Scoutmaster, will help you with these.

At some point, your Scout troop will likely go on a one-week camping trip in the summer, where you can use the knowledge and skills you've learned in your weekly Scout meetings at Mutual.

Every Church priesthood quorum has a president, two counselors, and a secretary—if there are enough boys in the quorum. The bishop will ask one of the deacons in your quorum to be the president. This deacon may be the oldest deacon, or it may be someone else. This is his calling, meaning his assignment.

The president will be asked to choose three deacons to help him as his counselors and secretary. These three have to be approved by the bishop. The bishop will lay his hands on the head of the president and set him apart to be the president. The bishop will also give the president priesthood keys—this means the authority to direct or make the final decisions about the work of the quorum. The bishop is the priesthood leader of the ward of Church members and he holds the keys to make final decisions about what happens in the ward. The bishop, or some other person chosen by the bishop, will put his hands on the heads of the counselors and secretary and set them apart for their callings, but they will not receive priesthood keys.

It is the duty of the quorum's president and his counselors (called the presidency) to plan the activities and work of the quorum. The president is not a king or dictator. In making plans for activities or work, the president should respect, talk to, and get ideas from his counselors and listen to the opinions of other members of the quorum before making final decisions.

When you are a new deacon, some of the older boys will probably be the president and counselors. They may ask you to do things to help with the work of God in the Church. Usually, you should do the things they ask you, but if you think they aren't treating you fairly, you can talk to your quorum adviser about it.

When all the deacons in the quorum respect the quorum presidency and cooperate with each other, the quorum can be peaceful, unified, happy, and successful in doing God's work. When you are older, you may be asked to serve as part of the quorum presidency. At that time, you will have to ask other deacons to do

certain tasks. You will want them to respect you and do what they are asked, so you should do the same when your quorum president or counselors ask you to do something.

Once each month, the deacons quorum president, the teachers quorum president, and one of the priests quorum assistants meets with the bishop, the ward Young Men and Young Women presidents, and the class presidents for the three Young Women's classes to discuss and plan the activities and work of the young men and women in the ward. This is called bishop's youth committee or BYC.

Some of the activities and work of the quorum might include planning visits to other deacons who are sick or who have been injured in an accident, young men who just moved into the ward, or young men who aren't coming to church to find out if someone hurt their feelings; doing a good turn for someone (meaning service projects); or planning a camping trip, a basketball game, a visit to a museum, or other such activities. There should be a balance between fun activities and work activities.

As a priesthood holder, you will have two private interviews each year. One of them will be with the bishop and about six months later, the other will be with the bishop's counselor. These interviews are to get to know one another better and become friends.

You can trust these men and tell them how things are going in your life and any problems you have. You can talk about your goals. They want to help you be successful and happy.

As a priesthood holder, you may be asked to give talks in sacrament meeting from time to time. This is to help you to become a good public speaker and learn how to express your ideas and thoughts to others. You should not be afraid of this. The talks you'll be asked to give will be short (five or so minutes), and you can get help from your parents and prepare at home before you give the talk.

On fast Sunday (the first Sunday of the month), if you want to, you can share your testimony of the gospel, like you see others do. Your testimony is your feelings about how the gospel helps you in your life. No one will make you share your testimony—it is only if you want to do it.

As you are twelve years old, you might want to begin reading the Church's magazine for youth called the *New Era*. Maybe you have read the Church's magazine for children called the *Friend*. The *New Era* has more grown-up articles and pictures for teenagers and youth.

Also, the Boy Scouts of America publishes a magazine for young men called *Boys' Life*, which is quite interesting. These magazines will come every month if you order them.

BECOMING A TEACHER

If you fulfill your duties as a deacon, when you turn fourteen years old, you can become a teacher. Just like when you received the Aaronic Priesthood, the bishop or one of his counselors will interview you privately to see if you are following the rules and commandments of Jesus Christ. If you are, your name will be presented to the Church members in a Sunday sacrament meeting, and they will be asked to raise their hands if they agree that you should be ordained to be a teacher.

If you are sustained (meaning approved) in sacrament meeting, then in a private meeting the bishop, your father, or someone else the bishop selects will place his hands on your head and ordain you to the office of a teacher in the Aaronic Priesthood. You can invite your parents and close friends to this as well.

When you become a teacher, you do not lose the authority you had when you were a deacon—you can still pass the sacrament, gather fast offerings, and help with taking care of the church building—if your priesthood leaders ask you to do so—but you get new authority.

Relating to the sacrament, a teacher can help to prepare the sacrament before the sacrament meeting for passing to the members. This means that if your teachers quorum president asks you to prepare the sacrament the next Sunday, you would come to church about thirty minutes before sacrament meeting starts and you would go to a small room near the sacrament table. There, you would wash your hands to make sure that they are clean.

Then you would wash and dry the trays for serving the bread and put one or two slices of bread on each tray—don't break the bread. You would put the sacrament cups in the water trays and fill the cups with water. You would put a first cloth on the sacrament table and put the trays of bread and water on the table. After that, you would cover the trays with a second sacrament tablecloth.

When you are asked to prepare the sacrament, another person will also be asked to do it with you so you won't be alone. You do need to ask your teachers quorum president or the adviser who should bring the bread to church. Maybe you'll be asked to bring the bread, or someone else will be asked to bring it. Because all the people who come to church that Sunday will eat this bread, it needs to be fresh and clean.

You should check to make sure the microphone on the sacrament table is working properly so that the congregation will be able to hear the sacrament prayers. If it's not working properly, you should tell your quorum adviser or the bishop or his counselor as soon as possible so they can get it fixed before sacrament meeting begins.

Right after the meeting ends, the teachers should go to the sacrament table, remove the sacrament cloth, and take the trays to the small room nearby. The water cups and the extra bread should be put in the garbage. The bread and water trays should be wiped off with a paper towel and put away in the cupboards so they will be ready for next week, or for the next ward's sacrament meeting that day. You should check the supply of sacrament water cups. If it's low, you should tell your adviser so he can get more cups before next week's sacrament meeting.

Another new thing that you can do as a teacher is become a home teacher. A home teacher is a person who visits members of the Church to make sure they are well and have the things they need. You will be assigned a companion who holds the Melchizedek Priesthood to go with you. You may be asked to visit several families each month.

At first, you may be shy, but as you visit various members and get to know them, they will become your friends. You may already know the families you are asked to visit from seeing them at church on Sundays, or you may know their children from the neighborhood or from the school where you go.

Home teaching is a way that God cares for all the members of the Church. If they have needs, their home teachers can try to think of ways to help them or report situations back to the bishop so he can ask someone to help them.

Jesus said we should love one another. Home teaching is one way that we do this. As part of the home teaching visit, you and your companion should share a gospel message; this means talking about some part of the gospel in order to remind the family to keep the commandments so God can bless them.

One of the special duties of a teacher is to be a peacemaker. If you know boys—especially boys who hold the Aaronic Priesthood—who are fighting or quarreling, you should try to help them to be friends.

Maybe by talking to them or by being a friend to both of them you can get them to be peaceful and be kind to each other.

Just like when you were a deacon, your teachers quorum will have a president (selected by the bishop), two counselors, and a secretary who have all been set apart for their callings. You should respect them and try to cooperate and help them be successful in carrying out the activities and work of the quorum.

On Mutual nights, you can keep working on your Scouting, including merit badges, progressing in the ranks on your way to Eagle.

Because you're older, as a teacher you will be able to attend stake activities, where young people from other wards come for activities, such as youth conferences, dances, singing, service projects, and sports activities.

Sometime in your last year as a teacher or your first year as a priest, you'll enter high school. In high school, you will have the opportunity to attend seminary. In some places where there are many Church members, you can go to seminary at a building near your school during the school day; in other places where there are not very many Church members, you will go to church early in the morning before school begins to go to seminary, or you will participate in a home study program.

In seminary, you will study the scriptures—the Bible, the Book of Mormon, the Doctrine and Covenants and Church history, and the Pearl of Great Price.

Be sure to continue to go with the youth of the ward on temple trips to do baptisms for the dead. Preparing for those trips and experiencing the Spirit you can feel in the temple will help your testimony become strong.

You will continue to have your yearly interview with the bishop and with one of the bishop's counselors six months later. Be sure and talk to them about how things are going in your life—they really care about you and have lots of experience and knowledge they can share with you.

BECOMING A PRIEST

If you fulfill your duties as a teacher, when you turn sixteen, you are eligible to become a priest in the Aaronic Priesthood. You will be interviewed in a private meeting by the bishop to ask about your worthiness, again pertaining to whether you're keeping the rules and commandments of the Lord. If you are judged worthy by your bishop, your name will be presented in sacrament meeting for a sustaining vote.

If approved, you will be ordained a priest in a private meeting. You can invite your family and close friends. The bishop, your father, or someone the bishop selects will ordain you.

As a priest, you will still have all of the powers, responsibilities, and authority you had when you were a deacon and a teacher. For example, you should still

go home teaching with your older companion. Sometimes, your Church leaders may ask you to help the deacons or teachers in their priesthood work or be a leader to them.

As a priest, you are in the priests quorum, which is a special quorum because its president is the bishop. In fact, *bishop* is an office in the Aaronic Priesthood, but he also holds the Melchizedek Priesthood. The bishop will choose two young men in the priests quorum to be his assistants.

In regard to the sacrament, now you will be able to offer the sacrament prayers on Sunday. These prayers, and the baptisimal prayer, are the only prayers we have in the Church that are written prayers, and Jesus Christ has told us to say them the same way each week. The prayers for the bread and the water are written on cards (they are in the scriptures too), and the priest saying the prayer reads from the card so that each word is correct.

Before sacrament meeting starts, the priests who have been asked to break the bread and say the prayers should wash their hands to make sure they are clean. When the sacrament song begins, the priests who are offering the prayers stand and remove the cloth covering the bread trays.

During the song, they break the bread slices into bite-size pieces to be passed to the members by the deacons. One of the priests kneels at the sacrament table and reads the prayer on the bread.

Afterward, he stands up, and the priests give the bread trays to the deacons to pass to the members. When the deacons bring back the bread trays, the priests offer the sacrament to the deacons and to each other, place the trays on the table, and cover them with the sacrament cloth.

Then they uncover the water trays. The other priest reads the prayer on the water, and the priests give the water trays to the deacons to pass to the members. Sometimes, if the priest saying the sacrament prayer makes a mistake, the bishop might ask him to say the prayer again. Don't be embarrassed when this happens; just read it again.

After both the bread and water have been passed to the members of the Church (and the deacons and priests), the priests put the trays on the table and cover them with the sacrament cloth. After the sacrament is completed, you should go to sit with your family for the rest of the meeting.

Some members of the Church may be ill or unable to come to Church on Sundays. They may ask the bishop to send the sacrament to them. The bishop or the Young Men president may ask you to take the sacrament to someone's home. You should go with another

priesthood holder, taking with you some bread, one of the bread trays, some cups, one of the water trays, and the Book of Mormon. (If another ward is meeting right after your ward and they need all of the sacrament trays, you should wait until all the wards have finished their sacrament meetings that Sunday before you take any of the trays.)

When you arrive at the home, you should make sure that the people understand that you are there to bless and pass the sacrament to them. You should kneel and read the sacrament prayers from the Book of Mormon (see Moroni 4–5) but replace *wine* with *water*, like in church, and then you and the other priesthood holder should pass the sacrament to the persons who have requested it. Sometimes, the people you are visiting will want to talk a little bit and will express their appreciation to you for bringing them the sacrament. Afterward, take the trays back to the church building.

As a priest, you are receiving more authority and trust from Jesus Christ and your Church leaders. After you have been ordained to be a priest, you have the authority to baptize, but remember that you need the permission of the person who holds the priesthood keys in your ward—that would be the bishop—before baptizing anyone. You also have the authority to lay your hands on another boy's head and give him the Aaronic Priesthood and ordain him to be a deacon, teacher, or priest, again after getting permission from the bishop.

Whenever you perform an ordinance such as baptism or ordaining someone to the priesthood, there should be at least two other people present so they can be witnesses that the ordinance was done properly. When you baptize someone, say the person's full name, and then say, "Having been commissioned of Jesus Christ, I baptize you in the name of the Father, and of the Son, and of the Holy Ghost, Amen." After that, the person being baptized must be immersed completely under the water.

Even though a person has been baptized, he or she can't become a member of the Church without receiving the gift of the Holy Ghost. Conferring the gift of the Holy Ghost can only be done by a man holding the Melchizedek Priesthood.

After a person has been baptized and received the gift of the Holy Ghost, the person's name is announced in a following sacrament meeting, and the members are asked to raise their hands to sustain him or her as a member of the Church.

If you are conferring the Aaronic Priesthood on someone, you should have him sit in a chair with his back to you, and you should have at least one other person who is a priest or who holds the Melchizedek

Priesthood join you in placing his hands on the head of the person.

If this person doesn't have the Aaronic Priesthood already, you should say the person's full name, and then say, "In the name of Jesus Christ and by the authority of the Aaronic Priesthood which I hold, I confer upon you the Aaronic Priesthood and I ordain you to the office of deacon." After that, you can say other things that would help the person to live the gospel and keep the commandments as you think of things to say, as inspired. You should end, "In the name of Jesus Christ, Amen."

If the person already has the Aaronic Priesthood, then you don't have to confer it on them, but instead you say, "In the name of Jesus Christ and by the authority of the Aaronic Priesthood, I ordain you to the office of teacher [or priest]."

Also, you should keep a record of the date and who was present. The record should be given to the bishop so that the ordinance can be filed away in the Church records.

On Mutual nights, your ward leaders may ask you to participate in the Venturing program, which is for older Scouts, or the youth may plan their own activities, such as career discovery, service projects, music, dance, drama, cultural events, sports or athletic events, and so on.

The Church leaders have asked young men and women not to date until they turn sixteen years old. So when you become old enough to become a priest, you can begin dating. The booklet *For the Strength of Youth* can teach you a lot about appropriate dating activities.

You should also continue to attend and participate in the seminary program, either at school, early in the morning at church, or in home study.

At this age, if you haven't done it previously, you should consider receiving a patriarchal blessing. Within your stake, there is a Church leader who has the special calling of patriarch. A patriarch is ordained to receive revelation for the members of the stake who come to him for a patriarchal blessing.

Receiving a patriarchal blessing is like receiving personal scripture. In the blessing, the patriarch will tell you the things that God wants you to know about yourself and how to live your life. To receive a patriarchal blessing, you should talk to your bishop. He will interview you and issue a recommend to receive your blessing. Then you make an appointment with the patriarch to meet with him.

When you go, you should dress in your Sunday best and pray before you go that the patriarch will be inspired by God.

As a priest, the Church asks you to attend a missionary preparation class. The purpose of this class is to explain more about serving a mission and to help you decide whether you choose to accept the call to serve a mission for the Church.

PREPARING FOR THE MELCHIZEDEK PRIESTHOOD

One of the most important parts of receiving and participating in the Aaronic Priesthood is that it then prepares you to receive the Melchizedek, or higher, Priesthood. There are three important responsibilities as an adult that require you to have the Melchizedek Priesthood.

The first responsibility is to serve a mission for the Church. Our prophet leaders have said that every young man who is physically and mentally able should serve a mission for the Church and have promised them great blessings if they do so. The second reason to receive the Melchizedek Priesthood is so that you can go through the temple to receive your endowment ordinance. Finally, the Melchizedek Priesthood will

enable you to go to the temple to be married and to preside over your family as a righteous man.

As you participate in the Aaronic Priesthood over the years, you will learn a lot more about each of these three things.

You should prepare for receiving the Melchizedek Priesthood sometime between the time you are eighteen and nineteen years old. If you are leaving for a mission, to attend college, or to work in a job, you should receive the Melchizedek Priesthood to bless your life. When the Melchizedek Priesthood is conferred upon you, you are ordained to the office of elder.

WHAT DO YOU THINK?

I know you can do it. More important, God, our Heavenly Father, and Jesus Christ, our Savior, want you to become a righteous man and worthy priesthood holder. God has told us that He will prepare a way for us to obey all of His commandments and rules—we just have to try to do the things He has asked us to do. This is called having faith.

As you do the things God has asked you to do, you will receive blessings that let you know your Heavenly Father and Jesus Christ care about you and are pleased with your good choices.

If you get discouraged, pray to God for help, read your scriptures to understand the gospel better and to gain hope, and talk to your parents, quorum adviser, or bishop to get counsel and ideas about how you can be successful.

Jesus Christ set up this wonderful Church, with lots of people and programs, to help us be successful. Only Satan wants you to fail, but you won't fail if you will follow God's plan.

You are a spiritual son of God. That means you are great, and if you follow the teachings of the gospel, you can also be righteous. That is the greatest thing we can learn to be in this life.

I pray God will bless you. Onward and upward!

Your older brother,
Tom Johnson

NOTES

_____

_____

_____

_____

_____

_____

_____

NOTES

NOTES

ABOUT THE AUTHOR

THOMAS E. JOHNSON is a former missonary for and bishop and stake president of The Church of Jesus Christ of Latter-day Saints. He is a grandpa who has five grandsons, whom he hopes will enjoy the blessings of participating in the Aaronic Priesthood, along with all the young men who read this book.

SCAN to visit

WWW.THOMASEJOHNSON.COM